GEO KIDS

Exploring The

URBAN ENVIRONMENT

By
Holly Duhig

BookLife
PUBLISHING

©2019
BookLife Publishing
King's Lynn
Norfolk PE30 4LS

All rights reserved.
Printed in Malaysia.

A catalogue record for this
book is available from the
British Library.

ISBN: 978-1-78637-438-7

Written by:
Holly Duhig

Edited by:
Madeline Tyler

Designed by:
Gareth Liddington

CONTENTS

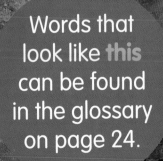

Push button
Wait for signal

Words that look like **this** can be found in the glossary on page 24.

EXPLORING THE URBAN ENVIRONMENT

Park!

Shopping!

My name is Nicole and I live in a city. I love living in the city. There's so much to see and do.

I'm doing a project for school all about different **environments**. My project is all about the urban environment.

GEO KIDS

Exploring The

URBAN
ENVIRONMENT

Nicole King's Urban Project

Urban means the town or city. Exploring the urban environment can be a lot of fun.

5

TOWN CENTRE!

I often visit the town centre at the weekends with my family. I can't wait to go to all my favourite shops. I have saved up lots of spending money by doing chores around the house.

We like to have lunch in the **square**. There are lots of pigeons in the square and they all want to eat our food!

There are also water fountains in the square. I love playing in them on hot days.

URBAN WILDLIFE

Baby Pigeons

I found this pigeon feather on a bench.

Some animals, like pigeons, love the city. They build their nests in high-up places like window ledges, rafters, beams and under bridges. When a baby pigeon poos in the nest, their parents don't get rid of it. It makes the nest stronger!

As well as pigeons, there are also a lot of foxes. They like to eat the food that people leave behind. We don't see foxes as much as pigeons because they are nocturnal. This means they sleep in the day and hunt at night.

Foxes eat rats too. This is helpful for cities because too many rats can cause problems.

This is hard to balance on!

After we go shopping, we sometimes go to the park. Cities have lots of parks to explore. Some have lots of green fields which are great for having picnics. Some have play areas.

There are lots of things to do in the park. You can take pedal boats out on the duck pond. There are lots of ducks, geese and even swans.

Ducklings!

Pedalos

11

POND WILDLIFE

There is a lot of frogspawn in the duck pond at the moment, so I wanted to learn more about it.

Frogspawn

Each black dot in frogspawn is an embryo that will become a tadpole. Only around five out of every thousand eggs will grow into adult frogs!

Frogspawn – As the embryo grows into a tadpole, it will eat the jelly around it.

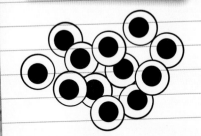

Tadpoles – The embryos grow a head, tail and gills.

Frogs – Adult frogs have a sac under their chin called a vocal sac. RIBBIT!

Froglets – The tadpole grows front and back legs – it's a froglet!

13

ROLLER SKATING!

There is lots of concrete and tarmac in a city, which is perfect for roller skating on.

There are lots of ways to explore the urban environment. There are trains, buses, trams and bikes, but I like to explore on my roller skates!

You can go to a skate park to roller skate. Some people go there to ride scooters and skateboards too. I love skating really fast up the sides!

Geo-Kid Top Tip!

Always wear a helmet, knee pads and elbow pads when you go roller skating.

MATERIALS IN THE CITY

Cement is mixed in a cement mixer.

Some skate parks are made from cement and concrete. Cement is made from rocks such as limestone and clay. It can be used to hold things together, such as house bricks. Concrete is made by adding sand, crushed rocks and water to cement.

Roads are made from tarmac, which is short for tarmacadam. It makes a smooth surface perfect for skating! Tarmac is made from sand and tar. It is very sticky when it's first laid down, but it soon dries.

CATCHING A TRAIN!

Geo-Kid Top Tip!

Stand well back from the edge of the platform when a train is on its way.

Other than skating, one of my favourite ways of getting around is by train. Some of the trains in my city go overground but some go underground.

I usually go on the train with my mum. Sometimes we have a snack or play **I spy**. I always sit in the window seat!

UNDERGROUND TRAINS

Most underground trains run on electricity.

96904

There are lots of buildings, parks and people in the city, so it can be difficult to get around quickly. Underground trains help people to travel straight from one part of the city to another.

To use the underground trains, you need to look at a map. First, you'll need to find which station you're starting at and which station you want to go to. You can then see which train line connects them.

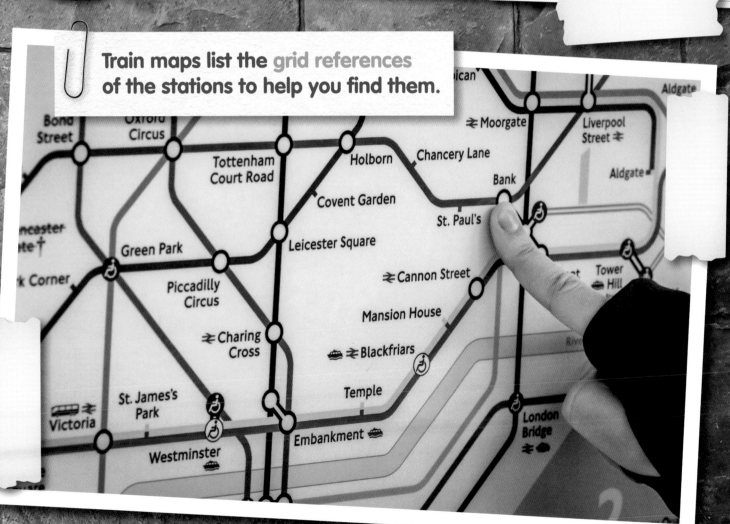

Train maps list the grid references of the stations to help you find them.

HEADING HOME

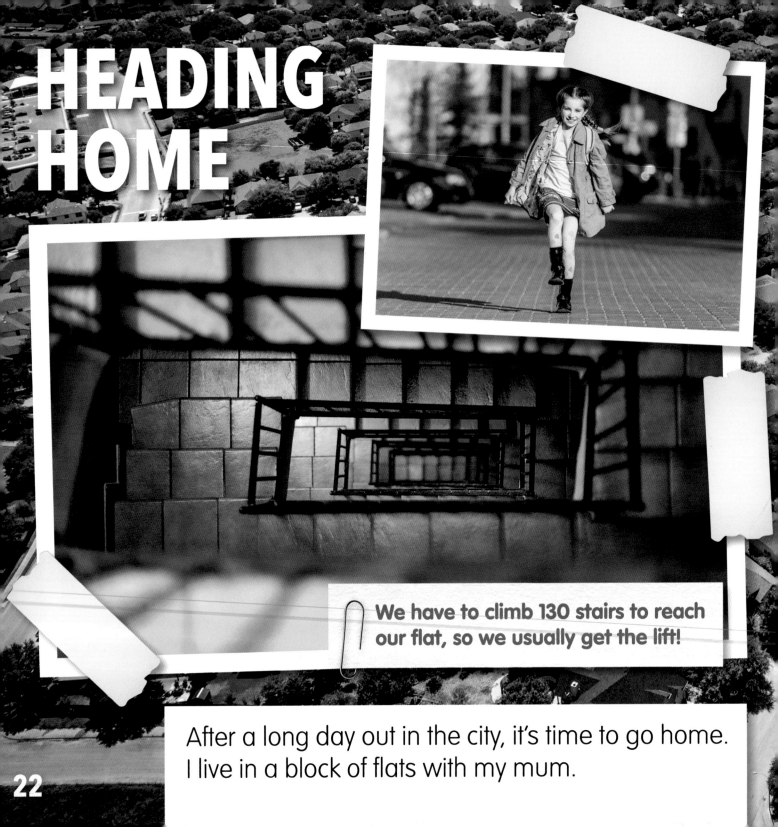

We have to climb 130 stairs to reach our flat, so we usually get the lift!

After a long day out in the city, it's time to go home. I live in a block of flats with my mum.

I've had lots of fun exploring the city but I'm glad to be home.

You can see all the way to the other side of the city from my bedroom window!

GLOSSARY

embryo	an unborn or unhatched young in the process of development
environments	the areas in which a human, animal or plant lives
gills	parts of an animal that let them breathe underwater
grid references	a letter and number that correspond to a location on a map
I spy	a guessing game where someone gives the first letter of an object they can see and someone else has to guess what that object is
life cycle	the changes a living thing goes through during the course of its life
limestone	a type of rock often used in building
rafters	large sloping pieces of wood that support a roof
square	an open public space at the centre of a town

INDEX